God

Smiled on This Jersey Girl

SUSANNE BRIGGS

Fulton Books, Inc.
Meadville, PA

Published by Fulton Books 2021

ISBN 978-1-63710-005-9 (paperback)
ISBN 978-1-63710-006-6 (digital)

Printed in the United States of America

Jesus Healed Me of Pancreatic Cancer

Around January of 2019, I was having a lot of pain in my abdomen and was feeling more tired than usual, and it was difficult to stay awake at work, so I made an appointment with my primary doctor. When asked if I could have a CAT scan to see what was wrong with me, he told me, "No, you don't need a CAT scan, I'm going to prescribe an anti-depressant for you because I believe you are having pains on the tiny nerves on the top of your skin, and the anti-depressant medicine is good for the nerves." I was appalled and told him I would not take that medicine and walked out of that office and never went back again.

Next, I went to my gastro doctor, and she put me on stomach medicine for thirty days and told me to come back after that if I still had pain. Of course, the pain was worse after thirty days, so I went back to her, and she performed an endoscopy to find out that my food was not digesting but just sitting on top of my stomach. She could not push the endoscopy bulb from my stomach into my small intestine. She still would not give me a CAT scan but told me to go on a liquid diet, and she was going to give me another endoscopy with a balloon and try to open that blockage to my small intestine. Just a few days before the next endoscopy was scheduled, I had jaundice. I had blood work done at my new family doctor's office, and I called my gastro doctor to let her know. She said to go and get a CAT scan immediately. The CAT scan showed I had a mass on my pancreas, and one of the gastro doctors (who performs this procedure in Jefferson Hospital in Philadelphia as well as New Jersey) performed a biopsy, and he also put a stent in my bile duct to stop the jaundice. The biopsy showed that I had pancreatic cancer. The tumor was pressing against my small intestines, and that is why I could not digest my food.

I made an appointment with an oncologist; she had me do six months of chemotherapy with the hope that it did and would not metastasize. The first chemo treatment went okay, but the second chemo treatment was horrible. I think what the doctors do is give you the strongest treatment possible to see if you can take it or not, and that is understandable because they want to get rid of the cancer.

However, during my second treatment, my tongue swelled up like a ball, and I was trying to tell the nurses to tell the doctor to come quick, but I sounded like Sylvester the cat. My son, Michael, was with me, and he scared me more by telling me that my tongue was getting bigger and bigger, and he said my tongue looked like a giant ball with smaller balls on the tongue. I thought I was going to die. Michael said to the nurses and doctor, "You know, the tongue doesn't stop in your mouth, it goes down to your esophagus," and that really put me in a panic. Years ago, I went into anaphylaxis shock from being allergic to penicillin and, again, a few years ago after I ate some weird bread; so naturally, I thought that was going to happen next, but it did not. The oncologist had the nurses put something in my port that calmed the reaction, and after the reaction went away, they gave me the second chemo. That chemo was hard too because a nurse from Jefferson Hospital would be there after I finished the treatment in the doctor's office and would attach a belt of chemo around my waist that she would attach to my port, so I had that chemo going into me for a couple of days, and then another nurse would come to my home and detach it. That chemo made me feel like I had no saliva in my throat, and my esophagus felt like it was closing. Plus, I was in the bathroom all day and night from it. I thought to myself, *I would rather die of cancer than go through this*. I called the oncologist and told her that the chemo was too strong for me, and I refused to take it again. She tried to talk me out of it, but I would not listen and told her that while on that horrible chemo, I had no quality of life whatsoever. I could tell she thought I was probably not going to survive without it, but I just could not take it and figured that at least I would be in Heaven soon if it did not work out. She started me on a new and easier chemo treatment. Thank God, my body accepted that treatment, and I felt as though I was getting healthier. All chemotherapies have their own side effects, but I was able to cope with the side effects of the new chemo treatment.

Meanwhile, I was on so many church prayer lists and have wonderful, dear friends that are prayer warriors. Even at my job, I had so many wonderful friends who were praying for me. They always sent me sweet cards and flowers. All that prayer and love gave me such a peace that Jesus loved me, and that I was in His hands no matter what. I started believing that He was healing me, and I tried to stay calm and just prayed constantly. I kept pushing the negative feelings away. Jesus's agonizing sufferings were on my mind a lot through all my treatments. Feeling His love is the most wonderful gift He has ever given me.

Over the next six months, I had many tests which included an MRI, a couple of CAT scans, and two PET scans which did show I had an artery from my pancreas that was encased with the cancer; however, the cancer did not metastasize anywhere else. My oncologist sent me to Jefferson Hospital in Philadelphia to see a surgeon (who specializes in the pancreas) to find out if I was a candidate for the Whipple surgery. He sent me for six weeks of radiation to shrink the cancer even more to make the surgery go better. My oncologist had me do six more weeks of just one of the chemotherapy drugs once a week that she said would work well with the radiation treatments. After the treatments were finished, I had another CAT scan and went to visit the surgeon again to talk about the surgery. He gave me the okay for the surgery, and it was scheduled for February 18, 2020. He explained to me and my sons how difficult the surgery is, and that it could take up to nine hours, especially if they had to replace an artery. I told him I believe that God is going to heal me, and that I was willing to go through it if it could make my life better. I just wanted to get back to work and live normally. He explained that during the Whipple procedure; they remove the pancreatic head, part of my small intestine, the gallbladder (my gallbladder was already removed years ago), and maybe the bottom of my stomach. He said in my case, they may have to harvest blood vessels from either my stomach or my leg or neck so that they can replace the artery that was encased with cancer, but they would not know for sure until they open me up. The surgical team in Jefferson Hospital is excellent, well respected, and I believed that I could trust them to do an excellent job.

All during my treatments, my two sons, Shawn and Michael, were like angels to me taking care of me, cleaning my house, and going food shopping when I was too weak to go out. In the beginning, when I was not eating, I was too weak to even stand up without holding onto my kids. They made me smoothies every day. After about one month of treatment, my oncologist told me to try to start eating again because my tumor markers were low, and she thought my tumor was shrinking. Right away, I was able to eat regular food again, and that made all the difference in my stamina, and I did not have to hold onto them to stand up and walk.

The surgeon wanted me to stay strong for the surgery, so I would walk a couple of miles every day. Before the surgery, I felt surprisingly good physically and spiritually, and I knew I was in God's hands and believed that He was healing me.

On February 18, 2020, my son Shawn drove me to Jefferson Hospital in Philadelphia at five o'clock in the morning to have the Whipple surgery, and I was praying for all of the surgical team. Most of all, I prayed that God would put His hands through their hands so the surgery would be perfect. The team was wonderful to me. I woke up in the recovery room at nighttime. I could not believe the pain I felt, it was extreme, but I saw my kids' faces looking down on me smiling, and that made me feel a little better. They told me the surgery went well. I must have fallen asleep for a little while longer, and when I woke up again, the pain was not as severe as it was when I first woke up. My surgeon came in to check on me, and I told him, "I believe God did a miracle and healed me." He said, "I think so too, and I'll tell you why, all of the edges of what we removed from you showed no cancer, but I'm sure if the pathologist chisels away at all of that, he'll find some cancer, but the edges look smooth which means we think we got it all." I asked him about the artery, and he said, "We did not need to remove it." But I was not fully with it because of the anesthesia, so I did not ask him anything else. Later I found out that they removed my pancreatic head, the bottom of my stomach, and some of my small intestine, and seventeen lymph nodes and two cysts on my kidneys.

A couple of weeks before my surgery, I asked my oncologist if I would have to worry about any of my insides melting together from the six weeks of radiation I had (I knew someone that had her intestines melt together from radiation a good many years ago), and she said not to worry because everything that was radiated would be removed by the surgeon during the Whipple procedure, so that is why I thought they removed the bottom of my stomach. The doctor explained to me that the pancreas is hiding behind the stomach, so it is in a tricky spot for the radiation, and the bottom of the stomach was affected by the radiation. There was no way to avoid the radiation hitting the stomach. I did notice during that time of radiation treatments that I did get nauseous, and my stomach hurt.

God's blessings were all over me during my stay at the hospital. I was in the recovery room for twenty hours because there were no beds, and the recovery room was packed with people, which was not fun, but my surgeon somehow got me in a beautiful suite that was reserved for VIPs or folks that donate to the hospital, which I was neither; it felt like a dream. The nurses were so wonderful to me. I remember hearing one of them say that I was their star patient but did not understand what they meant. Six days later, the surgeon came into my room to release me, and he said to me and my son, "Did you hear about the pathologist report?" We said no.

"They could not find one cancer cell in everything we removed from you, the chemo and the radiation must have knocked the cancer out of you. This happens to only 2% of the population." I shook my head no and told him that I believe I got a miracle and that God healed me, and the doctor agreed with me. Do not get me wrong, my oncologist and radiation doctors were great and did an excellent job, but we all know the stories of pancreatic cancer. I knew God removed it completely, and that He had something important for me to do. I honestly told all the doctors that I went throughout my treatments (and the surgeon) that I believed that I was going to get a miracle because I was on so many prayer lists. They probably thought I was nuts. The power of prayer is amazing.

My Dream of the Father Telling Me to Warn Them

Right before I got sick, I had an extraordinary dream that I was summoned up north to this particularly important place, and I found myself in this incredibly beautiful neighborhood that I thought was in northern New Jersey. I brought a friend with me, and we were passing these very beautiful mansions, and I commented on the fact that this must be the richest neighborhood in this state; and suddenly, I was at the address from which I was sent. As we went through this huge building, I noticed that the owner of this place really takes care of so many people. I commented that I just did not understand how he could take care of so many people, and that his place was big enough to hold all of them. There were countless rooms with plenty of space for everyone. I remember seeing three girls (who I thought were triplets) on a balcony with a banner hanging off it. Suddenly, I turned my head, and there was an older man with white hair and a beard, and he said to me, "There isn't much time, you have to warn them, you have to warn them." As I was agreeing with him, suddenly I woke up, but I felt as though the dream was really God the Father talking to me, and He wanted me to witness to whomever I could and help them believe in Jesus Christ, His precious Son, because that's the only way to get to Heaven. I remember feeling that my witness had been getting stale and old, and I needed to pray about being a better witness. Well, be careful about what you pray for because now I have a story to tell about the power of God, but it was hard to go through all of that, but if I can help one soul go to

Heaven, it's worth it. I have seen a lot of miracles in my life. Jesus said in John 14:1–4:

> Let not your heart be troubled; you believe in God, believe also in Me. In My Father's house are many mansions, if it were not so, I would have told you. I go to prepare a place for you. And if I go and prepare a place for you, I will come again and receive you to Myself; that where I am, there you may be also. And where I go you know, and the way you know.

You see, Jesus did not promise us a rose garden down here, but he did promise us one in Heaven.

I know Heaven is real, and that God the Father loves us so much. Jesus said in John 3:16, "For God so loved the world that He gave His only begotten Son, that whoever believes in Him should not perish but have everlasting life." I cannot stand the thought of someone not making it to Heaven. Hell is also real. Just the thought that I could have helped someone escape Hell, and I did not try to help them is too much for me.

Losing My Twin Sister

My twin sister Rosie got extremely ill the same time that I started my chemo treatments. She had COPD, and it was getting worse. About ten years before, she came down with pneumonia, and it ruined her lungs. I will never forget it because it was on Good Friday, and she had to spend Easter of that year in the hospital, and she loved Easter and getting together with family. We brought her up some Easter food, but I know she hated my cooking and was so disappointed that she could not cook because she was the best cook, and we all really enjoyed it. To me, cooking is a pain-in-the-neck chore. She went to different doctors and received a lot of treatments and was on a lot of machines. She started on oxygen and, eventually, had to use it 24/7. She struggled to even walk up the stairs. She was a fighter and kept going to work every day and doing other chores even though her body was not strong enough to do those things. She even took oxygen to work (she had an office job). Rosie loved her kids (she had two sons and two stepdaughters and four grandchildren), but she was too sick to do things with them; that broke her heart. In June 2019, it all just kept getting worse. She was in the local hospital and was put on a ventilator on and off. Her kidneys started to fail, and she had to go on dialysis, had terrible bedsores, and had multiple infections and fluid in her lungs.

Finally, the doctors performed a tracheostomy, and she could not communicate with us any longer, but at least she did not have that ventilator down her throat any longer. She was too weak to hand-write words or text; that was so hard to deal with. I was too sick to be there for her, and she was too sick to be there for me. It seems like for a few years before we were sick, she would tell me she was worried about getting too sick to work and too sick to cook and being invalid.

I always told her not to worry, and that I would take care of her and help her. We never dreamt that both of us would be so sick at the same exact time, making that promise null. After a while, I started to feel stronger and visited her when I could, but she got worse. My nephew Brian drove me and my brother Johnny and my sister-in-law Sharon to Temple Hospital in Philadelphia to visit her because the doctor said she was not going to make it through the night. We left a few hours before she died. She went to Heaven on November 22, 2019. I felt like my right arm was taken away, but I am happy for her that she is free from all the horrible suffering she went through. We all prayed so hard for a miracle for her to be healed, but she was not. I believe that God really did give her a wonderful miracle by taking her to Heaven, although I miss her every day, I am so happy she will never suffer again. Rosie was always the glue that kept our family together. She was one of the funniest, sweetest, caring persons that I ever knew. Everyone in the family and her friends miss her so much. I am so thankful to God that He gave me such a great person to be my twin sister. She is probably making the angels laugh every day, she is so funny.

I knew that God healed me for a reason, and that He had a mission for me, so I fought the sad, negative thoughts. There were times I thought how nice it would be if I died and could be with Rosie again, but I know God does not want me to think that way. We will be together in His time, not mine. I must focus on what He wants me to do on earth while there is still time. I believe we are living in the last days and must warn them as what was told to me in the dream. For us, our lives here on earth are just a drop in the bucket of time; eternity is forever and ever, without end. Maybe I can help the people I love and even strangers choose to spend eternity with Jesus in Heaven and escape Hell.

Because I have a port in my chest, it has to be flushed with saline solution at my oncologist's office, so I had to make an appointment with my oncologist. I asked her if she heard about my miracle (I always told her I would get a miracle), and she said, "No." I told her what the surgeon said to me, so she read the pathologist's report and looked shocked. She said she usually gives her patients that received the Whipple surgery six more months of chemotherapy, but she said that it is very rare for someone not to have any cancer cells left, so she made me get another CAT scan, and even though I knew it would not show any cancer, I let her do that so she would believe me. Of course, the CAT scan showed I do not have any cancer.

My Parents' Story

My mom and dad grew up in Philadelphia. My dad could not graduate from high school because his parents needed him to work since my grandfather suffered strokes, and my grandmother suffered from asthma. He had an older brother and sister. Both my parents lived through the Great Depression. My mom used to talk about her parents not having enough food for the family. Then along came World War II, and my dad served in the army and signed up for the Darby's Rangers and was seriously wounded while fighting in Italy. He spent two years in different hospitals undergoing many surgeries and almost lost his right arm. The doctors took a bone and ligaments out of one of his legs and somehow attached it to his arm. They then opened his right side and sewed his arm inside so it would all mend together. Of course, he suffered tremendously, but they did save his arm.

When my dad finally came home, he fell madly in love with my mom, and they married and had six children. Their wedding picture shows my dad in his army uniform and his arm in a cast. My dad always wanted to be a policeman and thought after the war he could do that, but his war injuries destroyed his dream. His brother and uncle were both Philadelphia policemen. He got a job (which he hated) in an office as an accountant clerk. My dad was the quiet, strong type. My mother loved to laugh and enjoyed her family; her siblings were all like that.

My mom was a great storyteller, and she told me that one day before she and my dad got married that they had an argument while walking down Market Street in Philadelphia, and she walked ahead of my dad because she was angry at him, and some guy whistled at my mom, and my dad punched him right in the face. It did not deter him that he just finished two years in hospitals and surgeries! My dad was always very protective of my mom. My siblings and I could not even give my mom a dirty look, because my dad would go ballistic on us. Oh, how he loved her.

My mother came from a big family; my grandparents had six kids, three girls, and three guys. All my aunts and uncles had a great sense of humor; they were all great storytellers. My mother was also a great cook, and she would always cook us a huge breakfast on Sunday mornings either before or after church. Every Sunday, she would cook pancakes and sausages or bacon and eggs and always gave me an orange. To this day, I always eat an orange every morning. We all loved her Sunday morning breakfasts (and everything else she cooked). Unfortunately, I did not get her cooking genes, but my sister Rosie did. Like I said, my parents lived through the Great Depression, and My mom remembered there was not enough food to go around. She appreciated having food to cook for the family.

My Childhood

My first real encounter with God was when my sister Rosie and I were preparing to make our First Holy Communion. We were very young. We had to attend classes to prepare us to receive the Holy Communion at the local Catholic Church. I do not remember what the priest said to us exactly, but after that, I felt that God was talking to me and I could feel His love for me. It was so wonderful that Rosie and I would hold hands and walk up to the church by ourselves, a little earlier than we were supposed to, and sit in the empty church and just talk to God and feel the Father's love. I still remember that secure feeling of God's love.

When we made our First Holy Communion, I had a growth spurt and was taller than all of the girls at that young age (now I am average height), and we had to walk to the front of the church two by two to receive our communion, but I was the tallest girl and had to walk in between two girls at the very back of the pack who were very short, and I just remember feeling like a freak. After that, I went through a time that I wanted to be tall because my mother was five feet eight.

A Stanger in a Foreign Place

Those young years when I entered school were very confusing to me and had me questioning why I was even here on this earth and how did I get here. Even though I loved my family, sometimes, I felt as though I was an alien in a foreign place. The world was a very scary place.

Rosie and I attended a Catholic School in Camden, New Jersey, in first and second grade. My two older brothers Tommy and Johnny also attended that same school. Rosie and I went into first grade when we were just five years old because they did not have a kindergarten class. We were so not ready for school and the mean teachers we had. I think my mother was just fried from all the kids and needed a break from us and pushed us into going to school early. We had to take public service buses, and I was never comfortable with that. They separated me and Rosie in the classrooms, so I was alone to find the correct buses every day after school. It is a miracle that Rosie and I got home safely every night because we were both extremely nearsighted, and we struggled to see the message the buses had in front of them. We did not even realize that we could not see correctly until a couple of years later when we had our eyes tested in public school. We thought everybody was seeing what we were seeing. I would always ask the bus driver if his bus was going to my town. There were so many buses that it seemed Rosie and I were rarely on the same bus. I do not remember ever seeing my brothers on the same bus after school. One day, I saw my reflection on the glass window of the bus as I sat next to the window and was thinking that I just did not belong, and I just felt fearful of everything but did not feel comfortable talking to anyone about those feelings. My parents were not the "tell me how you are feeling" type. The nuns were so strict. When I was in first grade, my teacher who was an older nun acted like she hated me. One day, she called me up to the board to print the letter *B*. I was so afraid of her, and I guess it was just nerves that I could not print the letter *B* the correct way that she wanted me to. Instead of connecting the two loops, I went down a little bit before I drew the second loop. She started to scream at me and smacked me across the face a couple of times, and I ran back to my desk to cry and put my face in my arms. She then was screaming at me to stop crying. To this day, I write backhanded, but I am right-handed. She really traumatized me. That summer, Rosie and I had to attend summer school for Reading, and my dad took us there. It was shocking to me that our teacher, the hateful nun, was acting so completely different to my dad, and she talked so nice to him and was smiling the whole time. She acted like a super nice person; that was the first and last time I ever saw her smile.

It was not all bad in the school. Rosie and I would always help clean up the lunchroom after spaghetti and macaroni day. That was our favorite lunch, they would put the fat macaroni in a bowl and cover it with spaghetti sauce; we loved it. We would collect the bowls and dishes and clean up the tables. We loved doing that because it gave us a little extra time away from the classroom.

Another surprise for me was that for some reason, I was chosen to crown the Blessed Mother in the May Day Procession. It must have been a random thing because I'm pretty sure the nuns did not like me; I cannot imagine one of them choosing me. I just thought, and maybe I was wrong, but I always felt they thought my family was too poor (we all had holes on the bottoms of our shoes, and we were always looking for hard pieces of cardboard to put inside our shoes to block out the cold and wet rain). Anyway, I do not know how or why I was picked to crown the Blessed Mother, but it was an honor, and my mother went to a florist and had a beautiful crown made with blue and white flowers. It was beautiful. I felt so happy that day.

My Mother's Story

My mother had to go to the hospital one day to have gallbladder surgery, and we kids were staying with different relatives and friends. I was sent to my grandmother's house who lived in Philadelphia. Her house was old but nice. They had a spiral staircase that we kids loved. We always thought that it was amazing that the steps were so little, and we were told that when the house was being built, the people were smaller and had smaller feet. None of our big feet fit on the steps properly. Next to her house was an alley that separated their house from a little parking lot. My mom had funny stories about her brothers regarding that alley.

My grandmother was a cleaning fanatic. Whenever I tried to talk to her, she was either praying or cleaning her spotless house. She would sit me in a chair in an upstairs bedroom next to the window that would overlook Spruce Street in Philadelphia and ask me to pray for my mother that God would heal her and help her to come home soon. I was so lonely for my family, even though I loved my grandmother. It was so quiet there and so loud at home, and I loved loud. I remember one of my grandmother's across-the-street neighbor was a Jewish woman who escaped Nazi Germany, and her name was "Goldie." She would yell from her second-story window to my grandmother, "Hi Anna," and then she would yell to me too. She is the only person I recall that ever talked to me while I was staying there. She was a very sweet person with a great accent, and I always loved to listen to someone speak with an accent, even when I was young.

When my mother was feeling better, it was time for me to leave Philadelphia! I was thrilled to go home with my parents and loud siblings. Once home and reunited, I remember there was a beauty parlor across the street from our house, and my mother told me and my sister she was going to get her hair done. When she came home from the beauty parlor, her hair was long and blonde and looked like Veronica Lake. When she left the room, I said to Rosie, "Isn't our mother beautiful?" She agreed. We were so happy to be home.

My Family

We grew up in a large Irish Catholic family. My parents had six kids. My twin sister Rosie was the comedian of the family and was always a great cook and a great storyteller. Johnny is the oldest and is fighting cancer as I am writing this book. A lot of folks are praying for him. His wife Sharon and their two kids, Brian and Janine, and grandchildren are taking good care of him.

Tommy, the second oldest, retired and moved down to Alabama ten years ago with his wife, Jackie, to be near their daughter, Amy, and her family. Tommy's daughter, Amy, has four children, and then she adopted an older child (he is sixteen years old now) from the Ukraine. When Amy and her husband, John, went to the Ukraine to adopt Michael, the lady at the orphanage warned them to hide their money on belts around their waists, so they did, and that amount was $20,000. They were told that they had to pay for the adoption by cash. While on a train ride to the orphanage, someone gassed their room while they were sleeping, and when they woke up, they realized that someone stole $500 from Amy's pocketbook, but the thief did not find the money that was needed to adopt the child because that was hidden under their belts around their waists.

My brother Tommy and Jackie took care of their grandchildren for Amy and John while they were gone. Amy came home on Christmas Eve night so she could be with her children and give them the Christmas presents she bought prior to her trip, and John stayed in the Ukraine waiting for the orphanage to release Michael. A couple of weeks later, John and Michael took a plane home, and Tommy and Jackie and Amy and her kids and their friends went to the airport to greet them with signs that read, "Welcome to the US and Alabama." Initially, Amy and John were going to adopt a child with

Down syndrome from Russia, but the president of Russia, Vladimir Putin, signed a ban on US adoptions of Russian children.

That adopted child, Michael, became a born-again Christian after a school friend asked him to go to his church with him. Then, a few years ago, Michael then told my brother Tommy about the church and Tommy asked Michael if he could go with him. Tommy loved the church and the pastor and became a born-again. Tommy is full of joy, and he told me that his daughter, Amy, not only saved Michael from an orphanage in the Ukraine, but he would not be saved if she had not done this kind act of adopting Michael, so she saved two people. That was God's plan. Tommy has worked with Samaritan's Purse and helps a lot of people from his church, even though he has had heart bypass surgery and back surgery. Tommy and his wife, Jackie, love their church, the pastors, and other members of the church, but most of all, they love Jesus.

We also have two younger brothers, Bobby and Jamie. Bobby loves to talk about Heaven. Bobby and his wife, Sue, have visited Tommy's church in Alabama and really liked it a lot. Their son, Jason, also moved to Alabama and works for the space program. Jamie is the baby of the family and is a sweet guy. They all have different personalities but all love to laugh, and they all love God and family. We grew up with a lot of laughter, but we all had fights at times, especially when we were young, but we all love each other. Johnny and Tommy were born in Philadelphia, and the rest of us were born in New Jersey. My parents were born and raised in Philadelphia.

From the time Rosie and I were born, until we were almost seven years old, we lived in an attached house in a small town called Woodlyn, New Jersey, that was not far from Philadelphia. The house was not the greatest and had a lot of huge ugly roaches. It did not matter how much we cleaned the house, and I helped my mother clean a lot; even when I was young, the roaches were still there. At night, I would always wake up and had to use the bathroom, but as soon as I would turn on the bathroom light, the roaches were all over the bathtub and the floor, and they would scatter. My dad finally bought an illegal rat poison and put it all through the basement. I always hated that basement; it was dark, and we had a big old coal burner that made scary noises. The next morning, my dad called us to come down the basement, so we went down the basement steps, and it looked like a black rug on the bottom of the floor; there were so many dead roaches. My dad cleaned it up and we never saw those ugly roaches again. Thank you, Jesus.

And then one beautiful day, we were all thrilled to learn that my dad bought a brand-new house for us in West Deptford, New Jersey; a three-bedroom split-level house with the GI Bill, and no one ever lived in that house before. We were going to attend public school, and we had to walk up the street to get there. No more public service buses! We thought we were rich! There was a big farm behind our house with cornfields and chickens. Rosie and I shared one bedroom, and Tommy and Johnny and Bobby shared another bedroom. Jamie was not born yet. My parents bought bunk beds for the boys and put a single bed in the same room for Bobby who was the baby of the family at that time.

The neighborhood was newly being built, and eventually, the farmer who owned all the property behind us sold the farm to the house developers. When we first moved in, there were just a few houses on the block, a few across the street, but boy, did those developers work fast. Soon there was house to house behind us and all down the streets. It was amazing how fast the neighborhood grew. When I was fourteen years old, Jamie was born. We were all protective of him since he was the baby, and he was so cute and sweet. My mother was so upset when she found out she was pregnant at age forty, but my baby brother brought a lot of laughter and joy to her and to all of us in the house. Again, that is God's plan.

We had a great neighborhood, and everyone was close with both my parents and us kids. It just seemed that we all had the same kind of personalities and humor. We had lots of fun pool parties (we had an above-ground four and one-half feet pool) and barbeques in the summer. My aunts and uncles and cousins were also close, and they all had a wonderful sense of humor, and they always had hysterical stories to share with each other. On fourth of July when I was a young teenager, so many relatives were in the pool because it was so hot, and the temperature was around a hundred degrees that the pool just exploded, and my baby brother, Jamie, was playing in his sandbox not far from the pool. The water just took him right through the white wooden fence and into the neighbor's yard. Everybody was upset that the pool was destroyed and concerned about Jamie, but they were also laughing hysterically because one of my uncles was such a funny person, and he was doing something like a stand-up comedian act. We just ate good food the rest of the day and enjoyed being with family. Jamie was fine, the sandbox acted like a little boat that steered him safely to shore, and eventually, my parents bought another pool because my Mother loved to go swimming just as much as the kids. Even my two boys, years later, learned how to swim in Grandma's pool. My family has a lot of fond memories of those pool days.

The Hayride

In 1963, my mother and other neighborhood parents thought it would be a good idea for the kids to go on a hayride on Mischief Night to keep them all out of trouble (we had a bad habit of soaping car windows on that night every year). I remember a time that we had to run all through the neighborhood trying to avoid the cops catching us, and somehow, we never got caught.

Anyway, the neighborhood parents hired a cowboy ranch in Washington Township, New Jersey, to give us a fun hayride. I recall that the hayride was not actually held on Mischief Night, but soon afterward, maybe the day after Halloween. The ranch was very authentic looking, the workers were real cowboys, and the horses were big and beautiful. My brother Tommy, our friend Marlene, my sister Rosie, and other friends all climbed up on one of the hayride wagons, but the ranch workers pulled me and a couple of my friends off the hayride because it was too crowded. They said, "Get on that last wagon." I was so upset. The wagons were going on a regular road with little lighting, I believe they had lanterns. The parents' wagon went first, and Rosie and Tommy's wagon went second, and my wagon was supposed to go last. My oldest brother, Johnny, was on the same wagon with me. The workers could not even attach the horses to that third wagon. They were jumping up on their hind legs and were making a frantic noise. The workers kept saying that the horses were spooked. The workers finally gave up because they could not get the horses to drive the wagon, and they just told us to go into the bar area and get hot chocolate and wait for the others to come back. We could not go home because the neighborhood parents drove us, and they were in the first wagon. My neighborhood friends, Billy and Jimmy, and I decided to run up the road and try to catch up to the second wagon, but we just could not do it. We thought we saw them afar off, but we ran out of steam. It was a chilly autumn night, and it did feel a bit eerie. I do not know if there were any streetlights, but I just remember it was so dark and cold on that road. We went back to the bar and drank the hot chocolate. A little while later, one of the boys that was on that second wagon came running into the bar, and he had blood on his clothes, and he said that the wagon was in a bad accident up the road, and that a car was going very fast and hit that second wagon. My mom was home that night because my baby brother got sick, and she did not want to leave him. She fell asleep on her bed next to my baby brother, and she dreamt that she saw two headlights coming toward her at a high rate of speed, and she heard a loud *thud*. She woke up very shaken.

After the accident, we thought it was amazing that Rosie told us that while on the second wagon, she stood up to see two headlights coming toward the wagon very quickly and she screamed, "Car," and then she heard a very loud *thud*. My mother heard a *thud* also in the dream she had.

My brother Tommy told me that he remembers flying in the air over the telephone lines, and he fell on a field that was freshly plowed. He said that because that field was freshly plowed, the field saved his life and others. Rosie woke up on the ground with a lot of the other kids all moaning and crying. One of the girls on her wagon was killed instantly; her name was Lois, and she was a very pretty fifteen-year-old girl. I did not know her very well. After school, a few days before the hayride, I remember running into her while walking down my street with some friends, and she was so excited to go on the hayride because it was going to be her first date. Her date was a cousin of two of my close friends, and I really liked him a lot and was happy for her.

One of our neighborhood friends, Debbie, was a tiny petite thing, and they found her on a tree just sitting on the big branch. She was okay though. My sister was hurt very badly with a fractured skull, and she had a fractured leg too because a huge board went right through her leg. My brother Tommy's leg was cut pretty bad, and he had to get a bunch of stitches, and our friend, Marlene, was hurt pretty bad. I remember one day after some time I was over at Marlene's house, and she had to go back to the hospital because she was bleeding from the wound she received from the accident. That wagon was hit with such force that the boards that the wagon was made from broke into pieces, and they were projectiles hitting everybody. There was another girl named Bonnie who injured her leg in the accident, and not long after the accident, her injury turned into a cancerous tumor, and the cancer took her life not long afterward. Right after the accident, a truly kind married couple who lived near the accident brought a lot of the injured kids inside their home to help them until all the ambulances came to take them to the hospital; they were two angels. Our neighborhood held a fundraiser to help that kind couple replace their rugs and furniture because everything was stained by blood in their house. The driver of the car was young and in the military. He was on a date and was very drunk. He said later that he never saw any wagon or any lights on the wagon. He was hurt too, but he recovered. I believe the girl that he was on the date with was all right.

My father was working late that night, so my uncle took my mother to the hospital to see if my sister was okay. My mom walked into the hospital at the same time as Lois's mother, and my mother was trying to console Lois's mother because she was crying, but neither of them knew at that time that she was dead. My mom saw someone take Lois's mother to a gurney, and that person lifted the cover and showed her Lois's lifeless body. My mother said she would never forget Lois's mother's loud cries when she found out that her daughter was dead.

One of the parents from the first wagon took me home, and I will never forget later that night sitting around our kitchen table and crying with my parents and others and talking about Rosie and Lois and the others, and I just could not stop shaking. Rosie had to undergo a lot of treatment for her injuries. She also had to have skin grafts to cover her scars. She went through a lot. She was in a wheelchair for a while, and then crutches.

I often wondered about that night, if those horses that were supposed to drive the third wagon would have been calm and cooperated with the workers, the car would have hit my wagon because that third wagon would have been in the back. When I became born-again, I realized that it was Lois's time to go to Heaven, and nothing was going to stop it. God has a plan even though we do not always understand tragedies like this; I trust in Him. Lois came from a Christian family and so did Bonnie. Lois's funeral was the saddest funeral. Her father cried the entire time I was there. It broke my heart, and we found out later that he did not want Lois to go on the hayride that night, and the last memory of her was them arguing about it. I do remember, that was the time I started to wonder a lot about death.

Then, President John F. Kennedy died later that month in 1963. My family loved him, and we were so sad watching the funeral on television. My mother got involved in politics around the time that he was a senator. We saw him in Trenton, New Jersey, at one of his campaign rallies. It was a beautiful sunny day, and Senator Kennedy was so handsome, and I loved his auburn hair, and he was sitting in a convertible and waving to us. We were able to get close to his car. After his death, I remember thinking about God and wondered about Heaven and Jesus, but I was a wild teenager and was drawn into the world. God was so patient with me.

Even though I was drawn to live a wild teenager life, I can remember—even as a teenager—sitting in church with my dad, and the church would get this golden tint to everything; it seemed that everything in the church was going to disappear, and I wondered if I was going to see something from God. This happened more than once. I do not believe I ever told my dad about that. Jesus always tugged at my heart, but I was running away from Him.

The Fall Down the Steps

When Rosie and I got older—and a little more worldly—we went away from God to do our own thing because we were too cool for God, or so we thought.

One summer night, when I was a teenager, I was wild, and all I wanted to do was party with my friends, and we were out drinking; I was very drunk, and my friends dropped me off at home. My parents were sleeping in their room with their very loud window air conditioner blasting, and Rosie was awake and tried to help me up the stairs, and when we got to the top, she said, "Are you okay," and I said, "Yeah." She let me go, and I fell backward onto a lamp and table. I cannot believe that my parents never woke up. Well, that fall started off years of pain in my tailbone. I went to a chiropractor, but I always left there in more pain. He took x-rays and said that my two bottom vertebras were pushing against each other, and I damaged my tailbone. The only way I could get relief from the pain was to lay on my side for some time, but the pain continued.

Married and Living
in a Commune

I got married to a man named Andy when I was twenty years old. We graduated from the same high school, and I see now that he and I were not ready for marriage. We were typical hippies and lived in a commune in New Jersey. My best friend from high school, Judy, was married to Andy's best friend, and they lived in the same commune. I was her matron of honor at her wedding. This lifestyle of living in a commune tore me and Andy apart. Having Judy there with me made it all okay though. Andy and I did divorce years later, but we remain friends.

Gave Jesus My Life

Andy was friends with a man named Howard who was quite handsome and looked like a guru with long blond hair, and he was attending Haverford College. He had been selling Fuller Brush products door to door. One day, Howard went to a house to try to sell the Fuller Brush products, and the woman opened the door and let him in. Her name was Jean, a devout Christian who happened to have the gift of prophecy. Jean also had visions, and she told Howard things that only Jesus would know about him, and she helped him and other friends to stop smoking pot and other drugs and turn to Jesus. Some of them claimed they saw visions of angels.

Howard introduced Andy to Jean, and Andy was trying to get close to God. One Saturday in October of 1971, Andy brought me over to Jean's house so that she could help me because he knew I was really a mess. I really wanted to meet her but was afraid that she would know all my horrible sins I committed, and don't you know, when I went over to her house, she talked to me for seven hours (which really felt like twenty minutes, and that's the truth) about all of the miracles that Jesus did for her. She told me that Jesus loved me so much that if I were the only person alive, he would still be crucified for me; that is what it means to have a personal relationship with Him. All my years, I thought you had to be Catholic or Methodist or Baptist to be saved but never knew that you just must have a personal relationship with Jesus to be saved. I asked her how can Jesus forgive me after all I have done? She did know the sin I was carrying around and said, "Jesus forgives you, and now, he wants you to forgive yourself and stop punishing yourself." As soon as she named my sin, I got hysterical crying and it was like all the pain and guilt was crying out of me, and Jesus's Holy Spirit, love, forgiveness, grace, and mercy were pouring into me. I could actually see and feel Jesus's golden love pouring into me. She said that Jesus wanted me to give Him my life, and I gave Him my life that day and have loved Him ever since. For the first time in my life, I felt so free of all I was holding inside. Jean told me later that she did not want to talk to anybody that day, but when she saw me sitting on her step, she knew she had to help me. Thank God, she did. I was truly "born again" when I left her house. Looking back, the saddest days of my life were when I was running away from God, and I was not living the way He wanted me to live, and the happiest days of my life are when I feel like I am right with God and living the way He wants me to live. It is a peace that passes all understanding.

Our Move to New York

Jean was helping other folks to come to Jesus, and one of them was named Steve, and he had other friends who were musicians who were music majors from Haverford College, and they started a band named New Zion. They were amazing musicians. Steve had a wealthy, generous wife named Vicki. She funded the renting of a beautiful, sturdy, old fashion house for the winter in upstate New York in a town named West Coxsackie so that the musicians could get their creative juices flowing, and they had a big old bus with "Zion" painted on the side. It snowed often up there. Steve hired Andy and one of our friends, Kevin, as their soundmen. There were the Bumpington's who did the electronic work. Charlotte was Kevin's wife, and she was pregnant at that time. The house was huge with many bedrooms and even had a sound room.

Andy and I had a beautiful bedroom. There were other couples, and most were musicians. Kate was a nurse who was also pregnant, and her husband, Gene, was the drummer. There was a couple of single guys in the band: one was named John who played the bass guitar, Darryl (not sure what he played), another musician named Ernie, and another sweet couple who I really liked a lot but can't recall their names. Steve wanted to rent his equipment out to other musicians to make some money. The equipment was state of the art. I remember one time they were negotiating with the group America to rent out their equipment to them, and some of our guys went to a concert for America, but their promotor made arrangements with someone else to rent equipment. Our guys enjoyed the concert anyway.

One day, two tall English guys from Liverpool, England, with long curly hair came into the commune, and they both carried guitars, and our musicians were all excited about them coming. They jammed in the music room together for hours. When they took a break, I made them a cup of tea and started to witness to both about Jesus, but it seemed that I spoke with one in-depth. I do not know if they were famous or if they were in a famous band, but the gentleman that I spoke with told me he was friends with George Harrison of the Beatles. I loved the Beatles when I was younger, especially Paul McCartney, and I saw "Hard Day's Night" nine times. He had my attention. For some crazy reason, he told me that the only thing his father does back in Liverpool, England, was watch the "telly." I thought that was hysterical for some reason and laughed out loud. He said, "How do you know that Jesus is really God? George Harrison thinks that his god is real." I was just a baby Christian at the time, but I answered him that I believe there is a heart-shaped void in each of us that only Jesus can fill, and when you accept Him into your heart, you will know it's been filled, and that Jesus is real, and there is no other God. We talked some more, and they went back to New York City where they were staying, but we never saw them again. I trust that God sent others to them, and maybe I just sowed a seed. Hope they got saved.

Jesus Healed My Back

One night, while still living at the Christian commune, I had a dream that my back was in agony, and in front of me was a statute of Jesus (growing up Catholic, I mostly saw Him as a statue), and the statue came alive, and His hands were so golden and warm and healing. He touched me, and all of the pain was gone in an instant. I was so thankful and did not want to leave Him, but He sent me to go and do His work. When I woke up, I was so disappointed that the pain came back later in the day. I told everyone in the commune about my dream, and later that night, they all laid hands on me and prayed for Jesus to heal my back. As they prayed for me, my eyes were closed, and I could feel Jesus's warm golden hands touching me, and He healed my back. God is so good.

Dream That God Talked to Me

Again, while at the Christian commune, I had a dream that Jean and her daughters took me to Heaven into the throne room, and there afar off was God the Father sitting on His throne. I could not see His facial features, but He looked very strong, and I remember He had crisscross sandals on his feet. Suddenly, Jesus was to the left of me, and He was so beautiful and kind, and we were just walking up to the throne, and I could not stop looking at Jesus. Suddenly, Jesus and I stopped walking right in front of the throne. I looked at the throne, and to my surprise, no one was there, and suddenly, the Father, with an extraordinarily strong voice, started talking to me, and I fell right on my face. All I remember is that the Father said, "You are earthy." His voice sounded like many waters just like the Bible says. I woke up and thought it was just a dream. Jean called the Christian commune from New Jersey that day, and I do not remember who she was speaking with on the phone, but Jean asked that individual to ask me if I had a dream God was talking to me. I was shocked.

Made Delicious Bread

While at the Christian commune, Kate and Charlotte taught me how to make the best bread ever. Charlotte gave me a wonderful gift; it was a beautiful big bread bowl. We all became close friends. I was never a great cook, but, boy, that bread came out of the oven so big and beautiful. It amazed me and probably everyone who knew me. It did not matter if I made white bread, wheat bread, rye bread, or braided bread; they all came out so beautiful and delicious, and the smell would make you so hungry. I felt as though it was a sweet, little gift from God.

Wanted to Go Home to New Jersey to Have Our Babies

Not only were Charlotte and Kate pregnant up in the commune, but I conceived my first son, Shawn, up there. As mothers, Kate and I wanted to go home to New Jersey and have our own homes, and we wanted to give birth to our babies in New Jersey, and we did not want to live in a commune again. My mother always said, "No two women can live under the same roof and get along with each other unless they're family." Most of us got along fantastically, and we all did our share of cooking and cleaning. We moved back to New Jersey, and my hippie days and living in a commune were gone, I was having a baby! Even though I would not change that time in my life for the world, I was so happy to be back home in New Jersey.

New Chapter of Serving the Lord

Once I was back home, Jean and I and became close, and her family became my family. Jean started a "Jesus Movement" in New Jersey in the summer of 1972 at one of the local churches, and the meetings were awesome! The meetings were open to young and old. There was an elderly man, who was a pastor, and his wife who attended the meetings, and we called him "Kid." He was always smiling. Different pastors attended the meetings to see what it was all about, but most of the attendees looked like hippies, and a lot of kids sat on the floor (unless they were lucky enough to get a fold-up chair). Jean would give an invitation to accept Jesus Christ as Savior at the end of the night, and so many young people came forward; it just took my breath away. Some were my friends like Tommy and Steve and a few others who rushed up to Jean after she gave the invitation, and Tommy lifted her up; he was so happy. It is funny that I remember Tommy about a year before that at a commune we stayed at in Salem, New Jersey, and it was Easter time. The movie *King of Kings* was on the television, and Tommy got so filled up, and he jumped up off the floor and said he got the chills from watching that movie. God was working on him then, and it was obvious to me. Some of the people that came forth after the invitation I never saw before, but God kept bringing them in, and the most special to me was my sister Rosie. She did not come forward that night, but she was so convicted when Jean said, "You people in the back [my sister was trying to leave], if you leave here tonight, you may never hear this message again. The time to accept Jesus is now. You could get hit by a car, none of us are promised tomorrow." Those words haunted Rosie. She knew that Jesus was real, and it was time to stop running away from Him. One night, a reporter from the *Woodbury Times* unexpectantly came in and talked to Andy and others. Andy told the reporter that taking drugs again would be like eating garbage, and that the best high ever is knowing Jesus Christ as his Savior. It was an incredibly special time in our lives.

Jesus Gave Me a Spine Adjustment

At the meetings, we were all so filled with the Holy Spirit, and it was truly praise and worship. One night, while we were at one of the meetings, I started feeling a little twinge of pain in my lower back and felt the Holy Spirit nudging me on to tell everyone how Jesus healed me while I was living in the Christian commune. I had not had any pain on my tailbone since He healed me, so I got up and told them all about my healing. In later years, I had a couple of instances of my back going out, but never that bottom tailbone pain since Jesus healed me.

After we left the meeting that night, I went back to Jean's house and fell asleep on Jean's couch, and I felt hands on my back pushing up and down my spine like I was at the chiropractor office, and it wasn't gentle—it was forceful enough that they pushed me a little. For some reason, I was not afraid but was giggly about it. I looked around, and there was no one there, and I realized that it was either Jesus, or He sent an angel to give me an adjustment. All I know is that I have never had that horrible pain in my tailbone again. Praise God!

Speaking in Tongues

We did so many fun things for the Lord that summer. Even though I was pregnant, I just kept pushing myself to do whatever the Lord led me to do. One night, Jean and I went to the Philadelphia Jesus Movement meeting in Germantown. What a night! The meeting was held in a large empty warehouse. They had a huge, young congregation. Everyone wore bellbottom jeans. There were two young people praying for another person who was kneeling on the ground with both his arms extending up to God, and he was praying, and Jean said to me, "Watch that guy," and to my total amazement, I saw the Holy Spirit descending on that guy that was on his knees, and he started speaking in tongues. I was freaking out. The Holy Spirit was in the shape of a white dove, and it resembled a picture on a cover of a music album I saw in Jean's house called "Maranatha." Some young people stood up and gave their testimonies of how Jesus saved them. It was very moving.

One day, there were quite a few of us sitting down at Jean's kitchen table in New Jersey, and as Jean was speaking about Jesus, each one of us started speaking in tongues, not all at the same time. God did pour forth His Spirit on us as it is spoken in the book of the Acts of the Apostles 2:17–21:

> And it shall come to pass in the last days, says God, That I will pour out of My Spirit on all flesh; Your sons and your daughters shall prophesy, Your young men shall see visions, and Your old men shall dream dreams. And on My menservants and on My maidservants I will pour out My Spirit in those days; And they shall prophesy. I

will show wonders in the heaven above And signs in the earth beneath: Blood and fire and vapor of smoke. The sun shall be turned into darkness, and the moon into blood, Before the coming of the great and awesome day of the Lord. And it shall come to pass That whoever calls on the name of the Lord Shall be saved.

It was wonderful. The power of God filled our lives that day. In the Bible, the book of 1 Corinthians 4–11 reads:

There are diversities of gifts, but the same Spirit. There are differences of ministries, but the same Lord. And there are diversities of activities, but it is the same God who works all in all. But the manifestation of the Spirit is given to each one for the profit of all: for to one is given the work of wisdom through the Spirit, to another the word of knowledge through the same Spirit, to another gifts of healings by the same Spirit, to another the working of miracles, to another prophecy, to another discerning of spirits, to another different kind of tongues, to another the interpretation of tongues. But one and the same Spirit works all these things, distributing to each one individually as He wills.

When my son, Michael, was about twelve years old, I had a bible study and prayer meeting for the kids in the neighborhood and invited some of Michael's friends. I was praying for one of the boys who was around sixteen years of age, and suddenly, he started to speak in tongues, and his eleven-year-old cousin interpreted what he said. She got very emotional and started to cry. That was their first experience with gifts of the Holy Spirit, and I think the experience frightened her because she could understand everything her cousin was saying, but the rest of us could not understand a word he said.

Their grandmother, who was a sweet Christian lady, was there also. My Michael still talks about that to this day, and he is now a man. It had such an impact on him. I love the scripture from the book of Acts of the Apostles 11:16 that reads, *"Then I remembered the work of the Lord, how He said, "John indeed baptized with water, but you shall be baptized with the Holy Spirit."*

One night, Andy and I brought a friend named Harold to visit Jean. We were all sitting around her kitchen table, and all of sudden, I started to hear what sounded like an orchestra tuning up, and it sounded like they were tuning up for a concert. I could hear the symbols and all types of instruments, and I looked at Andy and our friend Harold, and they were just listening to Jean, and finally, I asked them, "Don't you hear that music?" Andy and Harold said no, but Jean looked at me and said, "It's getting louder." We heard someone singing, and the music was getting louder and louder. Even though it was beautiful, I was a little scared because it got so loud.

Also, during that night, I saw what appeared to be the Book of Life, and it had little white wings on each side of the opened book. I saw the hands that carried the book, and they were beautiful. One of my brother's names was being handwritten in the book. The Lord filled me with his Holy Spirit so beautifully that night. I saw a vision of many people's faces, most I did not know who they were, but later through the years, I recognized some of the faces when I would meet people and talk to them about Jesus. That night when I went home, I was lying in bed, and I was scared to death to see visions when I was not with Jean. I even prayed to God, "Please don't let me see any visions when I am not with Jean." I do not know why I was so scared. When I was with Jean, I was never afraid to see anything from God, in fact, I would pray that God would let me see visions. As I got older and wiser, the Bible taught me through the years not to be afraid. In 1 John 4:18 it reads, *"There is no fear in love, but perfect love casts out fear, because fear involves torment. But he who fears has not been made perfect in Love."* God is love, and I am so thankful that He really did cast out my fear.

Philadelphia Jesus Movement Leaders' Luncheon

One day, Jean had a luncheon for the Philadelphia Jesus Movement leaders, and she made Spanish rice and other delicious food. So many more came to her luncheon than expected, and we were wondering if there was going to be enough food to go around. Jean kept telling me to add rice to a large pot she had. Somehow, God really provided, and there was enough food for everybody, and we were all happy and all had a good time.

We also got involved with a couple of other churches nearby. We tried to help the youth; some listened, some did not. We were always out doing street ministry and other fun things for the Lord.

Jean started a prison ministry, and we were all communicating with prisoners by mail, even on death row. Some of our men went to the Trenton State Prison in New Jersey to visit those prisoners.

I remember Andy and I went down to Ranch Hope, New Jersey, for boys to see if we could help the kids down there. The pastor was a great guy. He helped a lot of boys. Andy did whatever he could down there: construction of a new dorm and maintenance.

Jean got sick and could not continue the work for the Jesus Movement. Sick or not, she always helped a lot of people. It was just a new and different chapter in our lives.

Shawn's Miracle

In October of 1972, my first son, Shawn, was born. He was the cutest baby in the world and so much fun. He was healthy except for those nagging allergies. I told Shawn every day that Jesus loved him, and when he was nine months old, he pointed to a picture of Jesus that I had on my l living room wall and said, "Jesus." I was filled with joy because that is the first word Shawn said that was crystal clear, and then about an hour later, Jean came over for a visit, and she said, "Did Shawn say 'Jesus' today?"

When Shawn was a month away from four years old, he had a bad cold, and we called the doctor, but she said not to bring him in. Later that afternoon, his breathing was labored, so we took him to the emergency room at the local hospital. After taking x-rays of his lungs, the doctor said that Shawn had double pneumonia and had to be admitted. I called everybody I knew and asked them to pray and fast for Shawn because his lips and nails were blue from not getting enough oxygen, and I was so afraid that he was going to leave me and go to Heaven, so I just prayed nonstop. A wise person once told me that if someone is dying, and I want a miracle for that person, I should fast and pray.

I had a nurse friend who worked in the emergency room named Kate (she is the same Kate who was in the Christian commune with me). She was close friends with the doctors that were working in the emergency room, so they worked on him fast. They gave him inhalation therapy and put him in an oxygen tent. His little tummy was pounding up and down from the labored breathing. His pediatrician did show up and acted like he was going to die; she left and said there was nothing she could do for him. Meanwhile, I would not leave him but sat on the chair in his room. Kate came up to see us after her shift was finished and told me to stop crying because Shawn needed me to be strong, and then she gave me a shot to calm me down. I eventually fell asleep on the chair, and suddenly, I heard Shawn shouting, "Mommy, Mommy, Jesus took me to Heaven and gave me a treasure chest with a bunch of presents." Shawn was no longer blue, and his breathing was no longer labored. He looked all golden, and there was a beautiful mist in the room. Shawn's pediatrician came in the next morning and was shocked that he was so healthy. She looked at his nails and lips and said, "This is a miracle!" At that time, my sister-in-law was working for Shawn's pediatrician, and she was working that day, and the doctor told my sister-in-law that she did not think that Shawn was going to make it through the night. Shawn also told me that there was a sign stuck in the ground in Heaven, and he could not read it, but Jesus said, "Tell your Mommy the sign says 'No Trespassing.'" I believe Jesus said that so I would know He was not going to take Shawn from me.

Michael Was Born

Almost six years later, my second son, Michael, was born, and was also filled with allergies and asthma. Most of his young life had me on my knees praying for miracles. I cannot tell you how many times we ended up in the emergency room. Looking back on everything we went through, I am thankful to God for all the blessings, love, miracles, and healings He did for us. It's an old cliché, but I am not worthy! Thank you, Jesus.

When Shawn was a preteen, he came to me and asked if he could go down the shore with his best friend's family for the weekend. Somehow, I scraped up the money for him to go, but I was sad because I did not have money to take my kids on vacations. I talked to God about it before I fell asleep, and I am sure I shed some tears. As I fell asleep that night, I found myself walking on a boardwalk somewhere so beautiful, so breathtaking, that it suddenly dawned on me that I must be in Heaven because there is no place on earth this spectacular. At the end of the boardwalk, there was a huge mountain filled with rich green tropical trees with the most beautiful, vibrant, red, hot pink, orange, blue, purple, and yellow flowers bursting all over the sliced fan-like branches. To the right of the mountain, there was a spectacular cliff and a waterfall with colorful birds flying overhead. There was a sunny haze in the air, not hot, not cool, but it was just right. It reminded me of the Jersey shore just after sunrise. The feeling of perfect health possessed my body. As I walked toward the mountain, I noticed that people were walking toward me. Everyone was smiling at me, and they all looked vaguely familiar, but I could not quite figure out who they were. At any rate, they all looked happy and content, and they all looked at me like they knew me. I did not want to leave this perfect place, but somehow, I knew it was time to leave. So, I prayed to God, asking Him to let me remember this beautiful paradise after I awaken. It was becoming evident to me that I was in Heaven, although I did not see God or hear Him. I felt Him and knew He brought me to this paradise. He was with me and loved me as a daughter. The next thing I knew, I woke up and remembered the entire experience. I was happy and grateful that God, in lieu of a vacation down at the Jersey shore, took me on the most fantastic vacation of my life!

Bobby Was Healed

In February of 1975, one of my younger brothers, Bobby, was scheduled to have surgery to remove a hernia. He already had a hernia and surgery when he was much younger. One day, I was watching the *700 Club* on the Christian channel, and one of the people praying on the show had a "word of knowledge" and said something to the effect of, "You have a hernia and you are supposed to have surgery, but Jesus is healing you, you will not have to go through the surgery." I shouted out to God and said, "I claim that healing for Bobby, Lord!" and I immediately called my sister and told her the story and talked to Bobby and his now-wife Sue. When Bobby went to see the surgeon, He said, "You don't have a hernia, you don't need surgery."

I cannot tell you why God let me and my family have so many miracles and answered prayers, but maybe it's because He knows I love Him so much, and I have the faith that when I pray, he hears me and answers me, but I also thank God for unanswered prayers and trust in God because He knows what He's doing. I am no different than anybody else because I am a sinner just like everyone else.

Trip to Myrtle Beach

About fifteen years ago, my friend Marion asked me to ride with her to Myrtle Beach, South Carolina, to visit our friend Billy. We took my car, and I always had a fear of driving on highways in the rain, so I prayed every day before we went down there for God to not let it rain the entire time we were driving on highways. Well, we made it all the way down to North Carolina, and suddenly, the skies were pitch black, and it got very windy, and I told Marion about my prayers to God asking him not to let it rain for us. I asked Marion if she ever prays, and she said, "Yeah, once in a while," and I said to her, "Please pray now because God will definitely hear your prayers and stop the storm from coming on us," and don't you know, it did not rain, and the skies became clear again. We made it to our destination rain-free.

Marion and I are both Jersey girls, and in New Jersey, you are not allowed to pump your own gasoline, so we never did our entire lives, and when we got to Virginia, we had to fill the tank up, so we drove into a gas station. Marion and I were laughing at each other because neither of us was sure how to do this simple task, and just then, a funny thing happened. A car pulled up behind us in the gas station, and it had New Jersey tags on it, and out popped a couple of guys, and they said they knew we were Jersey girls from our license plate, and they knew we probably did not know how to use the pump and make the payment, and they helped us. Now, what are the odds that a couple of guys from New Jersey would pull into the same gas station as Marion and I were in and understood our dilemma without us even asking them to help. God always takes care of His children. We finally made it to our destination in South Carolina, and we had a very nice vacation with Billy who was an excellent host.

St. Paul Is Chosen

The Bible does tell us about Saul who was persecuting the church, and all of the Christians were afraid of him, and he consented to Jesus's first martyr, St. Stephen's death by stoning, and he was entering the Christians' homes and dragged them out and threw them in prison. Saul also got letters of permission from the high priests that if he found any Christian while he was on his way to Damascus, he could bring them back to Jerusalem bound up. As it reads in Acts 9:3:

> As he journeyed, he came near Damascus, and suddenly a light shone around him from Heaven. Then he fell to the ground, and heard a voice saying to him, "Saul, Saul, why are you persecuting Me?" And he said, "Who are you, Lord?" Then the Lord said, "I am Jesus, whom you are persecuting. It is hard for you to kick against the goads." So he, trembling and astonished, said, "Lord, what do You want me to do?" Then the Lord said to him, "Arise and go into the city, and you will be told what to do."

Jesus changed Saul's name to Paul, and he was a wonderful, bold witness everywhere he went and brought a lot of people to the Lord. He did suffer tremendously along the way. He was beaten many times, shipwrecked a few times, imprisoned, and put on trial, and finally, he was martyred. Some may ask, Why did God choose

Paul since he was hurting so many innocent Christians? As it says in 1 Corinthians 1:26–31:

> For you see your calling, brethren, that not many wise according to the flesh, not many mighty, not many noble are called. But God has chosen the foolish things of the world to put to shame the wise, and God has chosen the weak things of the world to put to shame the things which are mighty; and the base things of the world and the things which are despised God has chosen, and the things which are not, to bring to nothing the things that are, that no flesh should glory in His presence. But of Him you are in Christ Jesus, who became for us wisdom from God—and righteousness and sanctification and redemption—that, as it is written, "He who glories, let him glory in the Lord."

God loved Paul so much that he brought his spirit to the third Heaven and showed him things he was not allowed to talk about. As it reads in 1 Corinthians 2:9, "*Eye has not seen, nor ear heard, nor have entered into the heart of man the things which God has prepared for those who love Him.*" Paul knew what was awaiting him in Heaven. When others have asked me if I was afraid to die of pancreatic cancer, I would tell them that I am afraid of suffering, nobody likes to suffer, but I know that God will give me the strength to cope with whatever trial I am going to have to go through. However, I am not afraid to die because I know how the book ends (by that I mean the Bible), and I look forward to spending eternity in His glorious presence. You cannot change things by worrying, but you can change things by praying.

Years ago, I had a dream that my friend Jean and I were running through an open field, and it started raining, and then the rain turned into something that looked like black coal on us, and the coal started turning into fire, and then that fire turned to pure gold.

Just then, I saw different family members in cars driving around the storm, and they did not have to go through the fire. Jean and I saw a covered bridge up ahead and ran into it. All I could think of when I woke up is that line in a famous song: "Some by the fire, some by the flood, but all through the blood." Jean and I have both suffered through many trials over the years, and I think that God was showing me that in this dream. Not everybody suffers, but everyone must believe in Jesus Christ to be saved.

The Last Days

As I am writing this book, the coronavirus is killing a lot of people all over the world. Even my son, Michael, had a mild case. He is fine now, thank God. Michael's job has him transporting mostly seniors from nursing homes to dialysis treatments, bringing patients home from hospitals, etc. Michael was so afraid that he was going to get the virus and had to go on a ventilator that he thought about quitting that job. God was merciful to him by letting him get a mild case of the virus, and he did not have to go into the hospital or go on a ventilator. The dispatcher at his job asked him just the day before he got the virus if he would be willing to help the EMTs and transport two patients, that had the COVID-19, to the hospital. He said no because he was afraid that he would give the virus to me, and after undergoing all the treatments and surgery, he was afraid I would die. He got the virus anyway. It could have been a nightmare. Andy's brother, Lew, just died of COVID-19 after being in critical condition with the virus and was on a ventilator for thirty-nine days in a hospital in Vineland, New Jersey. He was a sweet guy and will be missed.

There have been horrific fires and floods and earthquakes and other apocalyptic events recently. On the news, I saw that huge locusts were destroying crops in Eastern Africa: countries like Kenya, Southern Ethiopia, Somalia, and others. On top of everything else, there are murder hornets that came from Asia to Washington state, and they are attacking the beehives and decapitating the bees' heads and destroying the entire beehive. They are also stinging people, and some folks have died because of the stings. Their stings go right through the beekeepers' suits.

A lot of people feel that something is just not right, and they are afraid of what is happening on the earth. I believe we are living in the last days, as Jesus talked about in the Bible, and I feel we do not have much time. In the book of Luke 21:11 reads, *"And there will be great earthquakes in various places, and famines and pestilences; and there will be fearful signs and great signs from heaven."*

But you do not have to be afraid if you know Jesus Christ, the King of kings and Lord of lords, the Alpha and the Omega. Maybe it is a wake-up call, and He is trying to wake up the world so they will turn to Him and be saved. Maybe He is saying that there is not much time. And in Luke 21:25–28, it reads:

> And there will be signs in the sun, in the moon, and in the stars; and on the earth distress of nations, with perplexity, the sea and the waves roaring; men's hearts failing them from fear and the expectation of those things which are coming on the earth, for the powers of the heavens will be shaken. Then they will see the Son of Man coming in a cloud with power and great glory. Now when these things begin to happen, look up and lift up your heads, because your redemption draws near.

An Invitation to You

I would like to finish this book with an invitation to accept Jesus Christ as your Savior to all the people who have not done so. There is only one way to get to Heaven, and that is by believing in and accepting Jesus Christ as your Savior. As Jean said to my sister Rosie, "You may never hear this message again, none of us are promised tomorrow." Eternity is forever, so please choose to spend it in Heaven with Jesus. All you must do is invite Him into your heart. He is knocking at the door of your heart, please let Him in. It is the best decision you will ever make. He died on the cross for you, and there is nothing more powerful than Jesus's blood that he shed on the cross for your sins and my sins. There is no sin that is more powerful than Jesus's blood, so do not think your sin is too horrible, and that you cannot be forgiven; that is why he died on the cross. The only unforgivable sin is rejecting Jesus. He loves you so much that He sacrificed Himself for you and me. We are all sinners, but Jesus loves us anyway.

All Heaven will rejoice when you accept Jesus as your Savior. Two thousand years ago, He left Heaven for you and for thirty-three years suffered so much. He paid the price for my sin and your sin. You may say that you are a good person, but that cannot get you into Heaven. Buddha cannot get you into Heaven, and either can Mohammed; they were just mortal men. Jesus healed the blind, the deaf, the lepers, the crippled, and all illnesses and even cast out demons from people, and he rose Lazarus from the dead after he was dead for three days. Jesus came down here to die for our sins so that we may spend eternity with Him. Jesus rose from the dead on the third day. That is love, and that is what God is. When you invite Him into your heart, He will wash away all your sins. You will find Him to be so forgiving, merciful, sweet, and full of love. He truly will set you free. John 8:36 reads, "*If therefore the Son shall make you free, you shall be free indeed.*"

In John 14:6:1 Jesus said, "*I am the Way, the Truth, and the Life. No one comes to the Father except through Me.*"

In the Old Testament, the prophet Isaiah prophesied the birth of Jesus about 700 years before Jesus was even born to the virgin mother. In Isaiah 7:14, it reads, "*Therefore the Lord Himself will give you a sign: Behold, the virgin shall conceive and bear a Son and shall call His name Immanuel.*" Immanuel means "God with us."

Also in the Old Testament, the prophet Isaiah also prophesied of Jesus, about 700 years before His birth, concerning the crucifixion: Isaiah 53:5–6 reads:

> But He was wounded for our transgressions, He was bruised for our iniquities, The chastisement for our peace was upon Him, And by his stripes we are healed. All we like sheep have gone astray; We have turned, every one, to his own way, and the Lord has laid on Him the iniquity of us all.

In the Old Testament, King David prophesied about Jesus's crucifixion in Psalm 22:12–18:

> Many bulls have surrounded Me; Strong bulls of Bashan have encircled Me. They gape at Me with their mouths, Like a raging and roaring lion. I am poured out like water, and all My bones are out of joint; My heart is like wax; It has melted within Me. My strength is dried up like a potsherd, And My tongue clings to My jaws; You have brought Me to the dust of death. For dogs have surrounded me; The congregation of the wicked has enclosed me. They pierced My hands and My feet; I can count all My bones. They look and stare at Me. They divide My garments among them, And for My clothing they cast lots.

King David was born in 907 BCE, and yet he foretold Jesus's crucifixion. That is the power of God.

I invite you all to come to Jesus. He loves you so much. He is wonderful.

About the Author

The author grew up in a large Irish family in New Jersey. She's an ex-hippie, a mother of two sons, a born-again Christian, and now a cancer survivor. She was shy as a child but grew out of that fast as she got older and became outgoing. Now she has a deep desire to reach out and help others by telling them the good news that Jesus loves them, and He is the greatest treasure she has ever found.

CPSIA information can be obtained
at www.ICGtesting.com
Printed in the USA
BVHW08012728042l
605943BV00008B/970